There Really
Was a Dodo

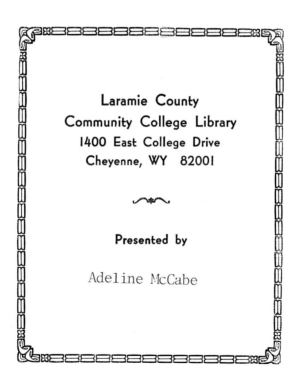

Esther S. and Bernard L. Gordon

THERE REALLY
WAS A DODO

Pictures by Lawrence Di Fiori

HENRY Z. WALCK, INC.
New York

*The authors wish to acknowledge the assistance rendered
by the following people in the preparation of this book:
Betty Haskell, Dick Wolfe, Myvanwy Dick and Joyce Fusaro.*

Text copyright © 1974 by Esther S. and Bernard L. Gordon
Illustrations copyright © 1974 by Lawrence Di Fiori
ISBN: 0-8098-1218-5
LC: 73-19252
Printed in the United States of America

Library of Congress Cataloging in Publication Data
Gordon, Esther S
    There really was a dodo.
    SUMMARY: Describes the dodo, who once flourished on
the island of Mauritius, and the reasons for this large
bird's extinction.
    1. Dodo—Juvenile literature. [1. Dodo. 2. Birds,
Extinct] I. Gordon, Bernard L., joint author. II. Di
Fiori, Lawrence, illus. III. Title.
    QE872.C7G67   598.6'5   73-19252
ISBN 0-8098-1218-5

To the memory of Jack Saranga. He left his "little dividends"—Jocelyn, Zimra, Sheryl, Dianne and Steven.

ONCE there really was a dodo. It was a strange, large bird that couldn't fly. But there aren't any dodos living on earth anymore, and there will never be another one. The dodo is extinct.

Dove

Thousands of years ago there were large birds, like pigeons, that had strong wings and beaks. Through the centuries, the birds evolved—they changed, little by little. Some developed into the pigeons of today, and some became doves. But others flew or were blown to the islands of Mauritius, Réunion and Rodriguez in the Indian Ocean. As years passed, these developed into a very different kind of bird.

Pigeons

On Mauritius, the birds had an easy life. There were many plants growing close to the ground that they could eat. And none of the other animals on the island needed to eat the dodos for food.

Slowly—over many generations—the birds began to change. Since food was so easy to find, they became fatter and larger. And since they hardly ever flew, their wings became smaller and weaker. Finally, their wings were no longer strong enough to lift the heavy birds off the ground. The dodos could no longer fly.

Once they couldn't fly, the birds weren't able to leave their island. But as long as they had no enemies, they were safe. They mated among themselves, and flourished.

These were the dodos—big, fat, yellowish-gray birds that weighed about fifty pounds each. Their heads were half-covered with feathers, so they looked as if they were wearing hoods. They had only three or four thick wing feathers. They used their sharp, hooked beaks to dig up roots which they ate along with seeds, plants and fruits. They swallowed stones and pebbles too, which helped to grind up the food in their stomachs.

A male and a female dodo would build a nest of grass and leaves on the ground. The female then laid one egg, about the size of a small grapefruit, and both birds took turns sitting on it until it hatched. The birds were very loyal to each other and to their chick.

Then in the early 1500's, the dodos' island was found by sailors from Portugal. Some Portuguese and Dutch ships stopped there during the next few years. When the sailors started exploring the island, the dodos' safe, easy life changed.

The sailors were looking for food. The other birds on the island—parakeets, shrikes and terns—were able to fly away and escape, but the dodo was helpless.

The dodos may not have been tasty, but they were fat and juicy. The sailors—who hadn't had fresh meat in a long time—caught and killed as many as they could. What they couldn't eat right away, they salted and took with them on their voyage.

The sailors also ate the dodo eggs. The birds tried to protect their eggs with their sharp beaks. But they were no match for the men armed with clubs.

No one is sure how the dodo got its name. The Dutch word "dodoor" means slow, and the Portuguese word "doudo" means silly, crazy or foolish. The dodo, with its fat body and waddling walk, was slow, and it looked foolish. The birds were given several names, but dodo is the one that stuck.

In 1644, people from Holland came to settle on Mauritius. They brought goats, pigs, dogs and cats, and these were new dangers for the dodo. Soon the animals ran all over the island chasing the slow, fat, flightless bird.

When the animals found one of the nests, they would chase away the dodos and eat the egg. So, with the nests destroyed and the eggs smashed and eaten, not many chicks were hatched. Every year there were fewer and fewer dodos.

When the sailors returned to Europe, they described the strange big birds that could not fly, and people wanted to see them. Several dodos were shipped back and shown in Holland, Germany, England and Italy.

All these dodos died. One of the dead ones was bought by John Tradescant who had a museum in London. He stuffed it and put it on display there, and it was later moved to the Ashmolean Museum at Oxford, England. After a while it was thrown out. Only the head and one foot were saved.

Meanwhile, the dodos on Mauritius completely died out. Records show that there were dodos there until 1681, but since that time no one has seen a living dodo.

After a hundred years or so, with no more living dodos, people started to think that there might never have been a dodo. They thought perhaps the dodo was only imaginary, like a dragon or a unicorn. The dodo head and foot were in the museum in England, but there was no full skeleton to show what the bird looked like or to prove that it really existed.

In Lewis Carroll's book *Alice In Wonderland*, which was published in 1865, a dodo appears. Alice meets the bird in Wonderland, and it gives her a thimble. But this didn't help to show that the dodo had really existed.

Dragon

Unicorn

Since then, people have gone to Mauritius to search for proof that the dodo was real. They have found bones buried in swamps and mud pools. Scientists have dug them up, examined them and put them together into dodo skeletons—proof that these birds really did exist. There are dodo skeletons in the American Museum of Natural History in New York City, the British Museum and the Paris Museum.

White Dodo

Solitaire

Scientists also found that there were two other kinds of dodos besides the one on Mauritius. The white dodo lived on the island of Réunion, and the Solitaire, another dodo, was found on the island of Rodriguez. Both kinds are extinct today too.

The dodo became extinct within about one hundred and fifty years from the time we first saw it. For hundreds of years before, the dodo had lived on Mauritius, Réunion and Rodriguez. But people and the animals they brought caught and killed so many dodos, and destroyed so many dodo eggs, that in a very short time, there were no dodos left.

Because of carelessness through the years, many kinds of birds and animals have become extinct. Today, the whooping crane, the orangutan and the blue whale are in danger of dying out. Our natural resources must be protected and used wisely. If our plants and animals are carelessly destroyed, we all may become as "dead as a dodo."